NURSE PRACTITIONERS GUIDE ON HOW TO START AN INDEPENDENT PRACTICE

~Veronica Mason DNP-FNP-BC~

Quanaah Publishing
www.quanaah-publishing.com

NURSE PRACTITIONERS GUIDE ON HOW TO START AN INDEPENDENT PRACTICE

©Copyright 2014

Quanaah Publishing

Written by Dr. Veronica Mason

Edited by Steven Napoli and S. Quanaah

Cover Design by S. Quanaah

-FOR TRAINING AND PUBLIC SPEAKING INFO-

Dr. Veronica Mason

EMAIL: Masonfamilymedicine@roadrunner.com

Printed in

The United States of America

For My Family
"But you are a chosen race, a royal priesthood, a holy nation, a people for his own possession, that you may proclaim the excellences of him who called you out of darkness into his marvelous light."

FOREWARD

Most Nurse Practitioner's long for autonomy, power to determine their own hours and the ability to make their own decisions. Unfortunately, the time it takes to start and manage a practice is extremely time consuming and the process can be complicated and over -whelming. Do you dream of having a pain center or a mental health clinic? Whatever your dream practice is, this book is a step by step guide to help you get started thru the complicated process. Remember, you are capable of achieving all of your dreams, **DESTINY IS NOT A MATTER OF CHANCE, BUT A MATTER OF CHOICE.**

I am honored to take the journey with you.

Veronica Mason DNP-FNP-B

INTRODUCTION

There are approximately 157,782 Nurse Practitioners worldwide in varying disciplines. (The Pearson Report The American Journal for Nurse Practitioners, March 2010). With the ever changing health care environment, Nurse Practitioners are at the forefront of becoming Independent Primary Care Providers. In the United States today there are 20 million Americans that are under- insured and 47 million who are not insured. American health care costs are rising at an alarming rate (much higher than inflation) and most American wages are not on the rise. This is a tremendous problem. To add insult to injury, most families that have insurance via an employee based health plan contribute an average of $43,281 a year and this is rising yearly at a tremendous rate.

Health care spending is currently 16% of the domestic product. It is projected to rise to 25% by 2030. In 2003, the United States spent $5,635 per person on health, more than twice the average within the Organization for Economic Co-operation and Development (OECD), an association of developed capitalist countries. In addition we are getting less for our money. The insurance companies are denying medications, test, and procedures for many Americans to decrease costs. In addition, they are requiring increases in co-payments, prior authorization for medications and test, and an increase in out of pocket expenses. Sadly, most American bankruptcies are due to medical costs. All the revenue spent on health care has not made us a healthy county. Obesity rates, diabetes, cancer, HTN, cardiovascular disease and life expectancy are unequal for each race.

Nurse Practitioners are in an excellent position to help in the current health care crisis. Where do Nurse Practitioners come into the picture with helping to improve the quality and access to health care for Americans? Nurse Practitioners can provide primary health care in varying disciplines for many Americans. Nurse Practitioners can provide quality health care at reasonable prices especially for the rural and minority population who in past history have had a problem gaining access to health care which is in line with the current health care reform policies. This population lacks trust in the health care system, but also have significant barriers such as transportation and belief systems which prevent them from accessing health care. However, this is not the only population we can help; Nurse Practitioners can treat patients in all disciplines and specialties.

The Nurse Practitioner Modernization Act is a pending legislation in the New York State Senate. The intent of the legislation is to end the requirement of a collaboration agreement between nurse practitioners and physicians as a condition for practice. This specific bill would amend the Nurse Practice Act Education Law of 1988 and would delete the requirements for collaboration agreements and practice protocols between Nurse Practitioners and Physicians.

Nurse Practitioners with solo practices, can design and manage clinics and offices that are unique in today's health care arena. These Nurse Practitioners can provide services that offer flexible hours, convenient locations with excellent access to care. WE must seize this opportunity to not only help the country but advance the profession, because remember we are all here for a reason and a mission.

I can accept failure, everyone fails at something. But I cannot accept not trying.
Michael Jordon

CHAPTER I

Success of a Nurse Practitioner private practice depends upon similar factors that determine general business success. Before we go any further I want you to take the time and do a self-assessment. Please use the work sheet below and list 10 reasons why you want to start your own private practice.

_____

_____

_____

_____

_____

_____

_____

_____

_____

_____

What are 3 things you would like to change about your current job?

_____

_____

_____

When deciding to open your own practice one should take an honest look at oneself to see if they have the qualifications needed to be an entrepreneur. Are you self-motivated? Do you mind being on call 24 hours a day? Do you mind working long hours Seven days a week? Are you able to handle stress and stressful situations? Can you handle not knowing if you will have enough revenue to pay yourself? If you do not think you are able to handle any of the above situations you may want to reconsider your decision to start your own practice. In any business venture not everyone is suited for entrepreuship abilities such as leadership skills, assertiveness, time management skills and negotiation skills are needed. Making money should not be the principle reason why you are considering starting your own practice. Helping patients achieve their health care needs in a spirit of excellence should be the ultimate goal. If you abide by this principle, the patients and the financial resources will come. Running a practice is a business and it can be done efficiently and profitably. After you have done your self-assessment and you believe starting your own practice is your dream, then you can move onto the next step. In addition to the self-assessment you should know what your strengths and weakness are to better manage your business. Please list below strengths and weakness.

Strengths

_____

_____

_____

_____

_____

Weaknesses

_____

_____

_____

_____

_____

CONFIDENCE

After years of working as a Nurse Practitioner I have come to believe that the main reason that prevents aspiring NP entrepreneurs from starting their own practice is confidence. NP's believe they don't have the resources, knowledge or support to be successful. You are a highly educated NP with specific expertise. You have your own unique talents and abilities.

Now that you have determined your strengths and weaknesses you can either go to your local business development center and get free training or hire outside side help in the areas that you are weak in. Consult your local Score business workshop which could be invaluable to you. They offer pre- business workshops and continued seminars for business owner. Score also offers a seminar on counseling and coaching with a person in your field you are considering starting your business to guide and help you thru the process.

It is also important to consider the impact starting your own practice will have on your family. Please consider the following: income, hours, and support level and how these will impact your family. I would recommend the marketing, financing, financial management, personnel, EMR courses at the local SBA (small business administration).

Income: start up business don't generally make money in their first 5 years, you must consider how you will support your family during your initial years. **Hours**: staring a practice will call for a tremendous amount of time to be invested by the owner. You must consider this before starting the business. Get your family involved in the decision making and make them aware what will be expected of you during your crucial first years. **Support level**: when starting you own practice you will experience isolation and loneliness. It is essential for you to talk with your family and friends and significant others. They, of course, have as much riding on your practice as you do.

DREAM/VISION

Your dream and vision for your practice must be specific and clear. Do you want to specialize or have a general medical practice? You must determine this, your target markets, as well the difference you want to make in health care.

What is your target market?

_____

_____

_____

_____

Who do you want to help?

_____

_____

_____

_____

What difference do you want to make in health care?

_____

_____

_____

_____

Name 2 goals you would like to accomplish within the next 3 months for your business.

_____

_____

Name 2 goals you would like to accomplish within the next 6 months for your business.

_____

_____

Name 2 goals you would like to accomplish within the next year for your business.

_____

_____

INTERVENTION	DATE ACHIEVED
Strengthens	
Weaknesses	
Consider impact of family	
Discuss hours, income & support with family	
Contact local SBA Contac local SCORE	
Take pre-business courses	
Goals	
Vision	

It always seems impossible until it's done.
Nelson Mandela

CHAPTER II
State Regulations

State Regulations & Scope of practice for Nurse Practitioners vary greatly by each state. Each state regulates care provided by Nurse Practitioners. In many states NP's work completely independently and autonomously of Physicians, while in other states a collaborative agreement with a Physician is required for practice. In New York State NP's require a collaborative agreement with a Physician (please see a copy of the documents required in New York State, Appendix A). Nurse Practitioners in States that require you to have a collaborative physician must secure a collaborative Physician. A collaborative agreement generally helps you define and guide your practice. The agreement should include all the required New York State information, as well as the specific tasks and duties of all parties involved including on call duties, review of medical records, and of disagreement resolution. In New York State Collaborators must review 1-2 NP's records at least every three months. In addition the agreement should include resolution of disagreement of any kind, including treatment.

Nurse Practitioners are also required to identify a protocol text from their states approved list as your official practice protocol. It which must reflect the specialty area of practice as identified on your State Education Department issued Nurse Practitioner certificate. The approved protocol texts include provisions for case management, diagnosis and treatment of pathology in the specialty area. Additional protocols or textbooks which may be appropriate to the practice and/or employment setting may be used but need not be reflected in the collaborative agreement (please see New York Sates Approved list Appendix B)

The National Provider Identifier initiative was mandated in New York State by the Health Insurance Portability and accountability and Accountability Act of 1996 (HIPPA). This Act requires that all health care providers apply for a National Provider Identifier (NPI) that will be used in all electronic health care transactions. The NP will be utilized by all health plans and health care clearinghouse to handle all claims and transactions. Nurse Practitioners can apply for an NPI by going to www.cms.hhs.gov/nationalProvIdentstand. Applications can be submitted online or via regular mail.

Each NP should contact their perspective Department of Health agencies to see what is required for them to start their practice please see the list below(please see Appendix C):

Locating a collaborative physician can be a difficult task. This is due to the lack of knowledge physicians have regarding NP's as well as their fear of malpractice liability by the NP. It may be helpful for you to advertise in your local paper, physician journals, nursing boards or online advertisements. The cost of paying a collaborator will vary depending on the complexity of the collaboration, but ultimately the decision will be a joint one between both parties. This can be done by paying an hourly or flat rate to the collaborator. You can also trade services. For example, you know a physician that needs a Nurse Practitioner for on call duties once a month or to work in his practice one or two days a month. You can negotiate, and instead of getting paid you can exchange services for him being your collaborator. I suggest that you become your own advocate. You know what your strengths and weaknesses are. Sell yourself!!! Before signing any legal contract you should consult an attorney. All documents should be mailed to your Department of Health, as well as kept in your office for review by the Department of Health.

In addition NP's would need to complete the practice protocol form from the Department of Health. This form requires the NP to select a practice protocol from the approved list by the New York State Education Department (Appendix B).

Please be aware that in New York State a physician cannot enter into agreement with more than four NP's. This is to ensure that appropriate monitoring can be performed by the physician. However there is no limit to the number of agreements an NP may have with different physicians. Please make sure you review your states regulations.

Please list any potential collaborators below.

_____

_____

_____

_____

_____

_____

_____

_____

Worksheet for CHAPTER II

INTERVENTION	DATE ACHIEVED
Review State Regulations	
Contact local state agency for forms	
Collaborator secured(in states which require)	
Collaborator agreement signed	
Practice protocol signed	

Far better is it to dare mighty things, to win glorious triumphs, even though checkered by failure... than to rank with those poor spirits who neither enjoy nor suffer much, because they live in a gray twilight that knows not victory nor defeat.

Theodore Roosevelt

CHAPTER III
DEA

DEA The Controlled Substances Act (CSA) was enacted into law by the Congress of the United States as Title II of the Comprehensive Drug Abuse Prevention and Control Act of 1970. The CSA is the Federal drug policy under which the manufacture, importation, possession, use and distribution of certain substances is regulated. The Act also served as the national implementing legislation for the Single Convention on Narcotic Drugs. The Drug Enforcement Administration (DEA) is a law enforcement agency under the United States Department of Justice, tasked with combating drug smuggling and use within the United States.

The scope and extend of prescription coverage a Nurse Practitioners has is also regulated by each individual state. In many states Nurse Practitioners have full prescription authority including schedule II. In other states, Nurse Practitioners are unable to write pain medications or schedule II. In the states that permit Nurse Practitioners to have full prescription authority, the Nurse Practitioner will need a DEA number in order to write scheduled medications including pain medications. A Nurse Practitioner must apply for a DEA number through the federal agency, which will allow them to write all medications which are on the market. In addition on April 19th 2011, President Obama signed into legislation the new REMS policy which requires all providers to be educated on safe prescribing and dispensing of extended release opiates. All drug manufactures must provide the educational materials to the providers. In addition New York States has a New Prescription monitoring program which requires all providers to access the PMP before any scheduled medications are issued. Please see below the New York State application web site for DEA Licensure. Please be aware that applying for a DEA number will take up to 2 months and requires Documents to be sent to the federal government. The cost for new applications is $390

you can apply online at www.deadiversion.usdoj.gov or by mail or phone at:

United States Department of Justice

Drug Enforcement Administration
99 10th Avenue
New York, NY 10011
Phone 877-883-5789, 800-882-9539 or 212-337-1593
Fax 212-337-2867 or 2895

Prescription Forms

If you satisfy all requirements for a certificate as a Nurse practitioner, you will be authorized to issue prescriptions pursuant to Section 6902 (3) (b) of the Education Law.

New York State Prescription Forms may be obtained from:

New York State Department of Health
Bureau of Narcotic Enforcement
433 River Street, Suite 303
Troy, NY 12180
Phone 866-811-7957 or 518-402-0708

Please see the list of DEA offices in your area (Appendix D)

Worksheet for CHAPTER III

INTERVENTION	DATE ACHIEVED
Contact local DEA agency	
Determine what NP's can prescribe in your state	
Apply for DEA license	
Read REMS policy	

In order to succeed,
Your desire for success should be
greater than your fear of failure.
-Bill Cosby

CHAPTER IV
Transcription

With today's ever increasing utilization of the computer and the internet, a healthcare provider must decide if they will do EMR (electronic medical records) or not. Electronic medical records are the latest tools providers are utilizing to ensure that their notes are legible. In addition you can do a variety of things with EMR, such as fax prescriptions to pharmacies, hospitals and other health care providers. You can have your labs, toxicology screens sent directly to your EMR software and they will be easily accessible with EMR. Please do your homework before purchasing any software as there are many EMR tools on the market, varying in price and features. Please make sure training is included in the package so you and staff can be trained on the software. A start up Nurse Practitioner practice may not have the funds to go paperless initially, but in time you will. Transcription is a very important factor in a medical practice that does not have EMR. You must ask yourself:

What kind of charts will you have?

_____

_____

_____

_____

Will you dictate all or part of your medical notes?

_____

_____

_____

_____

How will you keep track of your ordered labs?

_____

_____

_____

_____

If you decide to dictate your notes you will need to find a local transcription company or individual to transcribe your notes.

Worksheet for CHAPTER IV

INTERVENTION	DATE ACHIEVED
Determine your transcription needs	
Contact & interview local transcriptionist	

We can achieve what
we can conceive and believe.
-Mark Twain

CHAPTER V
Billing

How will you obtain your money after you have provided services? Will you hire a company or do your billing yourself. If you are a startup business provider and have never done medical billing, I recommend for the first couple of years that you hire a professional billing service that is familiar with your specialty. This will cost you a portion of what is collected. Some companies charge 8% of all monies collected, but the peace of mind is immeasurable knowing that the billing is done professionally and correctly. However, if you know someone or have worked with someone that has years of experience in medical billing for your specialty, you can hire them to do your medical billing. Remember, billing is one of the most important things in your practice. If your billing is not correctly done, your practice will not have the finances to run your office successfully. Be diligent about hiring the correct person for your billing services. Always get references from companies and call them up and speak with them. Some states have enacted rules that are requiring medical offices to start billing electronically. Example New York States has given Providers until 2015 to start billing electronically for their services; they will impose a fee after 2015 if their bills are not submitted electronically.

What type of billing service will you utilize?

_____

_____

_____

_____

Call 2-3 billing services in your area who specialize in your field of practice? What are their

fees?

_____

_____

_____

_____

Worksheet for CHAPTER V

INTERVENTION	DATE ACHIEVED
Determine billing needs	
Contact local billing agencies	
Interview billing agencies	

All the significant battles
are waged within the self.
-Sheldon Kopp

CHAPTER VI
Corporations

Anyone who operates a business alone or with others may and should incorporate. Any size business can benefit from incorporation. However, you must decide what business structure you will utilize and whether you will you incorporate or not. In New York State medical practices are considered professional corporations. Your attorney and tax advisor will be equipped to direct you in the exact business structure you should utilize. The advantages of incorporation are the ability to protect you from personal liability. Let's review incorporations:

Professional Corporation (PC) is a corporation of professionals. In some states some professionals are permitted to form a corporation under specific regulations, to allow the professionals to have the benefit of a corporation while meeting ethical requirements. The professional corporation does not shield professionals from personal liability resulting from his or her actions, but it does allow shareholders or directors to be protected from the actions of others.

General Corporation this is the most common corporation structure new businesses start. A general corporation is protected from the creditors of the business. A stockholder's personal liability is usually limited to the amount in the corporation and no more.

Advantages

1. Owner's personal assets are protected from the business debt and liability.

2. Corporations do not extend beyond the illness or death of the owners.

3. Tax Free benefits such as insurance, travel, retirement plan deductions.

4. Transfer of ownership facilitated by sale of stock.

5. Change of ownership need not affect management.

Disadvantages

1. More expensive to form than proprietorship or partnerships.

2. More legal formality.

3. More state and federal rules and regulations.

Citation: www.morebusiness.com/getting-started/incorporation/d934832501.brc

S Corporation

Many entrepreneurs and small business owners are partial to the S Corporation because it combines many of the advantages of a sole proprietorship, partnership and the corporate forms of the business. S Corporations have the same basic advantages and disadvantages of General Corporation with the added benefit of the S Corporation special tax provisions. When a standard corporation makes a profit, it pays a federal corporate income tax on the profit if the company declares a dividend; the shareholders must report the dividend as personal income and pay more taxes. S Corporations avoid this "double taxation" because all income or loss is reported only once on the personal tax returns of the shareholders. However, like standard corporations, the S Corporation shareholders are exempt from personal liability for business.

Limited Liability Corporation (LLC) LLC's combine many of the advantages and disadvantages of general corporations. LLC owners can have the corporate liability protection for their personal assets from business debt as well as the tax advantages of partnerships or S Corporations. A Limited Liability Company (LLC) is a business structure allowed by state statute. LLCs are popular because, similar to a corporation, owners have limited personal liability for the debts and actions of the LLC. Other features of LLCs are more like a partnership, providing management flexibility and the benefit of pass-through taxation.

Owners of an LLC are called members. Since most states do not restrict ownership, members may include individuals, corporations, other LLCs and foreign entities. There is no maximum number of members. Most states also permit "single member" LLCs, those having only one owner.

Advantages

1. Protection of personal assets from business debt

2. Profits/losses pass through to personal income tax returns of the owners

3. Great flexibility in management and organization of the business

4. LLC's do not have the ownership restrictions of S Corporations making them ideal business structures for foreign investors.

Disadvantages

1. LLC's cannot exceed 30 years

2. Some states require at least 2 members form a LLC

3. LLC's do not have stock and the benefits of stock ownership

Citation: www.morebusiness.com/getting-started/incorporation/d934832501.brc

Research Business structure.

_____

_____

_____

Type of business structure needed.

_____

_____

_____

Contact various lawyers on pricing for incorporation.

_____

_____

_____

Creating a Business Name

You need a Business name to follow through with the business structure. The options for business names are endless. Pick a business name that reflects the type of medical office you will have.

Write 5 possible business names here:

_____

_____

_____

_____

_____

When you set up your business structure your attorney will obtain a federal identification number for you. If you prefer to fill out the application yourself you can go to irs.gov and mail or fax it to the IRS Service Center in your state. You can also apply by phone by calling 1-800-829-3676.

Worksheet for CHAPTER VI

INTERVENTION	DATE ACHIEVED
Determine corporate structure	
Contact attorney to incorporate	
Create a Business name	

Failures are finger posts on the road to achievement.

C. S. Lewis

CHAPTER VII
Business Plan

A business plan is a great opportunity to work out a plan for your business. Banks require a business plan for financing, but even if you are not going to apply for a business loan a business plan is good to have. Most local stores such as Wal-Mart, Kmart, and Office max have business plan starter disc, that will walk you step by step through your business plan. It will not be an easy or quick task but it will help you look at your business from a different view. A business plan will force you to think about staffing, finances, marketing, budget, and revenues for the next twelve months. Remember, all bank loans require a business plan.

You can also get help with developing a business and other business related activities from your local SBA office. Please see the list of local SBA offices in your area (Please see Appendix E). I think this is a good opportunity to discuss strengths and weaknesses. Let's look at the **SWOT** analysis. SWOT is an acronym for Strength, Weakness, Opportunities, and Threats.

Strengths: what you do best at, where you excel your resources and / or experiences
Weaknesses: what you do poorly, what you lack, what is not working well
Opportunities: what opportunities are coming your way and where do you see potential?
Threats: what could get in the way, what obstacles or problem do you foresee?

INTERNAL	STRENGTHS	WEAKNESSES
EXTERNAL	OPPORTUNITIES	THREATS

INTERVENTION	DATE ACHIEVED
Obtain business plan maker from local store	
Start developing business plan	
Contact local SBA for help creating business plan	

All Things Are Possible To Him That Believeth
-Mark 9:23

CHAPTER VIII
Taxes

Every business is required to file taxes. Each quarter business taxes need to be paid and, according to your state, you will need to obtain an EIN number and federal tax identification number. You will have to contact your local IRS agency to obtain applications for these numbers. To obtain a SS-4 for federal tax I.D number in New York State you can call 1-800-829-3676. or go to their web site: www.irs.gov/smallbiz To obtain a NYS tax number call 1-800-462-8100 or go to their web site: www.nystax.gov for form DTF-17. To obtain information regarding NYS permits and incorporation call 1-800-342-3464. To file corporations with the Secretary of State, send documents to: NYS Department of State, Corporations & State Records Division, and 162 Washington Ave, Albany, NY 12231. The above information is for New York state residents only. You must contact your local IRS agency for more information (Please see Appendix F)

Worksheet for CHAPTER VIII

INTERVENTION	DATE ACHIEVED
Contact your local IRS	
Fill out forms for EIN#	
Fill out form for NYS tax # **Contact local tax advisory for advise & tax preparation help**	

CHAPTER VIIII
Supplies

You must determine your personnel needs, when starting a practice, you must figure out how many employees you need and their salaries. You can contact your local department of labor, local papers, and craigslist list.com for candidates. In addition you must determine how you will market your business. You must also know your budget for marketing. Every business needs a marketing plan, to reach your sales goal. Here is a question you will need to ask:

How you will advertise Online; Cable/TV; Newspaper; Local town paper; Health Care magazines; Local gyms; Fliers? Remember you are a new practice and you must get your name out be creative!

_____

_____

Here is a list of things you may need to start your own practice. This is not a complete list

1. Collaborator

2. Office location

3. Lights, cable, heat, electric

4. Computers

5. Phones

6. Printer

7. Fax machine

8. Business account

9. Exam table

10. Stethoscope

11. BP cuff

12. Chart files

13. Tuning fork

14. Needles

15. Syringes

16. Chairs/Furniture

17. Workers compensation insurance

18. Insurance for the contents inside the building

19. Disability insurance

I learned that courage was not the absence of fear, but the triumph over it. The brave man is not he who does not feel afraid, but he who conquers that fear."

Nelson Mandela

(Sample) Collaborative Practice Agreement

This agreement sets forth the terms of the Collaborative Practice Agreement between (nurse practitioner and specialty as listed on the State issued certificate) and (name of collaborating physician and specialty if any) at (name and address of agency or entity where practice takes place). This agreement shall take effect as of (date).

Introduction
(YOUR NAME RN, NP) meets the qualifications and practice requirements as stated in Chapter 257 of the Laws of 1988 and Article 139 of the Education Law of New York State, holds a New York State license and is currently registered as a registered professional nurse in good standing, holds a certificate as a nurse practitioner pursuant to Sec. 6910 of the Education law and herein meets the requirement of maintaining a collaborative practice agreement with (NAME OF COLLABORATOR, MD/DO) a duly licensed and currently registered physician in good standing under Article 131 of the New York State Education Law.

I. Scope of Practice
The practice of a registered professional nurse as a nurse practitioner may include the diagnosis of illness and physical conditions and the performance of therapeutic and corrective measures including prescribing medications for patients whose conditions fall within the authorized scope of the practice as identified on the college certificate. This privilege includes the prescribing of all controlled substances under a DEA number. The nurse practitioner, as a registered nurse, may also diagnose and treat human responses to actual or potential health problems through such services as case finding, health counseling, health teaching, and provision of care supportive to or restorative of life and well-being. This practice will take place at (above identified agency) or in such other facility or location as designated by (name of identified agency) or by the parties of this contract. The following exceptions to the certified scope of practice have been agreed upon by the undersigned parties: (list exception(s).

II. Practice Protocols
The protocols used in this (identify specialty as listed on State issued certificate) practice are contained in (name approved protocol text with all bibliography citations) and in (cite location of any other protocols which are germane to this particular practice).

III. Physician Consultation
The parties shall be available to each other for consultation either on site or by electronic access including but not limited to telephone, facsimile and email. Each party will cover for the other in the absence of one of them or (names of third parties) who are designated by (YOUR NAME, RN, NP and NAME OF COLLABORATOR MD/DO) as appropriate for coverage in the absence of

both parties. In the event that there is an unforeseen lack of coverage, patients will be referred to the appropriate emergency room.

IV. Record Review

A representative sample of patient records shall be reviewed by the collaborating physician every three months to evaluate that (name of NP)'s practice is congruent with the above identified practice protocol documents and texts. Summarized results of this review will be signed by both parties and shall be maintained in the nurse practitioner's practice site for possible regulatory agency review. Consent forms for such review will be obtained from any patient whose primary physician is other than (name of collaborating physician).

V. Resolution of Disagreements

Disagreement between (name of nurse practitioner) and (name of collaborating physician) regarding a patient's health management that falls within the scope of practice of both parties will be resolved by a consensus agreement in accordance with current medical and nursing peer literature consultation. In case of disagreements that cannot be resolved in this manner, (name of collaborative physician's) opinion will prevail. In disagreements between the nurse practitioner and non-collaborating physicians, the collaborating physician's opinion will prevail.

VI. Alteration of Agreement

The collaborative practice agreement shall be reviewed at least annually and may be amended in writing in a document signed by both parties and attached to the collaborative practice agreement.

VII. Agreement

Having read and understood the full contents of this document, the parties hereto agree to be bound by its terms.

Nurse Practitioner (Specialty):
Printed Name_____ RN license #_____
Certificate #_____
Signature_____
Date_____

Collaborating Physician:
Printed Name_____ MD license #_____
Board Certification_____
Signature_____
Date_____

Appendix B
Nurse Practitioner: Approved Protocol Texts

American Academy of Pediatrics Staff. (2008) *Pediatric primary care: Tools for practice.* Elk Grove Village, IL: American Academy of Pediatrics.

American Academy of Pediatrics. (2009) *2009 Red book: Report of the committee on infectious diseases* (28th ed.). Elk Grove Village, IL: American Academy of Pediatrics

American Psychiatric Association Staff. (2000) *Diagnostic and statistical manual of mental disorders, DSM-IV-TR: Text revision* (4th ed.). Arlington, VA: American Psychiatric Publishing, Inc.

Barkley, T. W., & Myers, C. M. (2007) *Practice guidelines for acute care nurse practitioners* (2nd ed.). Philadelphia, PA: Saunders [Imprint].

Boynton, R. W., Dunn, E. S., Stephens, G. R., & Pulcini, J. *(2009) Manual of ambulatory pediatrics* (6th ed.). Philadelphia, PA: Lippincott Williams & Wilkins.

Burns, C. E., Dunn, A. M., Brady, M. A., Starr, N. B., & Blosser, C. (2008) *Pediatric primary care* (4th ed.). Philadelphia, PA: Saunders [Imprint].

Camp-Sorrell, D., & Hawkins, R. A. (2006) *Clinical manual for the oncology advanced practice nurse* (2nd ed.). Pittsburgh, PA: Oncology Nursing Society.

Chan, P. D., & Johnson, M. T. (2009) *Treatment guidelines for medicine and primary care* (11th ed.). Mission Viejo, CA: Current Clinical Strategies Publishing.

Cloherty, J. P., Eichenwald, E. C., & Stark, A. R. (2008) *Manual of neonatal care* (6th ed.). Philadelphia, PA: Lippincott Williams & Wilkins.

Cooper, D. H., Krainik, A. J., Lubner, S. J. & Reno, H. (2010) *Washington manual of medical therapeutics* (33rded.). Philadelphia, PA: Lippincott, Williams and Wilkins.

Dickey, R.P. (2010). *Managing contraceptive pill patients* (14th ed.) Dallas TX: EMIS, Inc.

Donn, S. M. (2003) *The Michigan manual of neonatal intensive care.* Philadelphia, PA: Hanley & Belfus [Imprint].

Dossey, B. M., & Keegan, L. (2008) *Holistic nursing: A handbook for practice* (5th ed.). Sudbury, MA: Jones & Bartlett Publishers, Inc.

Dunphy, L. M., Winland-Brown, J. E., Porter, B. O., & Thomas, D. J. (2007) *Primary care: The art and science of advanced practice nursing* (2nd ed.). Philadelphia, PA: F. A. Davis Company.

Eagle, K. A., Baliga, R. R., Armstrong, W. F., Bach, D. S., & Bates, E. R. (2008) *Practical cardiology: Evaluation and treatment of common cardiovascular disorders* (2nd ed.). Philadelphia, PA: Lippincott Williams & Wilkins.

Fauci, A.S. (2011) *Harrison's principles of internal medicine* (18th ed.).New York, NY:McGraw-Hill Professional.

Ferrell, B. R., & Coyle, N. (2010) *Textbook of palliative nursing* (3rd ed.). New York, NY: Oxford University Press, Inc.

Gibbs, R. S., & Danforth, D. N. (2008) *Danforth's obstetrics and gynecology* (10th ed.). Philadelphia, PA: Lippincott Williams & Wilkins.

Gonzalez, R.,& Kutner, J.S. (2007) *Current practice guidelines in primary care 2008.* New York, NY: McGraw-Hill Companies.

Goroll, Allan H [Editor] and Mulley Albert G [Editor] (2009) *Primary care medicine: office evaluation and management of the adult patient.* Phildelphia, PA: Lippincott, Williams & Wilkins.

Hanks, G., Cherny, N., Christakis, N., Fallon, M., Kaasa, S., & Portenoy, R. (2009). *Oxford textbook of palliative medicine* (4th ed.). New York, NY: Oxford University Press, Inc.

Hawkins, J. W., Roberto-Nichols, D. M., & Stanley-Haney, J. L. (2008). *Guidelines for nurse practitioners in gynecologic settings* (9th ed.). New York, NY: Springer Pub.

Hay, W., Levin, M., Sondheimer, J., & Deterding, R. (2010). *Current pediatric diagnosis & treatment* (20th ed.). New York, NY: Lange Medical Books/McGraw-Hill, Medical Pub. Division.

Hazzard, W., & Halter, J. (2009). *Hazzard's geriatric medicine and gerontology* (6th ed.). New York, NY: McGraw-Hill Professional.

Heath, Cathryn B. (Editor), Sulik, Sandra M. (Editor) (2010) *Primary care procedures in women's health.* Springer.

Kennedy-Malone, L., Fletcher, K. R., & Plank, L. M. (2004) *Management guidelines for nurse practitioners working with older adults* (2nd ed.). Philadelphia, PA: F. A. Davis Company.

King, T. E., & Wheeler, M. B. (2007) *Medical management of vulnerable and underserved patients: Principles, practice, and populations.* New York, NY: McGraw-Hill Medical Pub. Division.

Kliegman, R.M., Behrman, R.E., & Jenson, H.B. (2007) *Nelson textbook of pediatrics* (18th ed.). St. Louis, MO: Elsevier Health Science.

Lewis, K. D., & Bear, B. J. (2009) *Manual of school health: A handbook for school nurses, educators, and health professionals* (3rd ed.). St. Louis, MO: Saunders.

Lovell, W. W., Weinstein, S.W., & Morrissy, R.T. (2005) *Lovell and Winter's pediatric orthopedics* (6th ed.). Philadelphia, PA: Lippincott Williams & Wilkins.

MacDonald, M.G., Ramasethu, J., & Vargas, A. (2007) *Atlas of procedures in neonatology* (4th ed.).Philadelphia, PA: Lippincott Williams & Wilkins.

Martin, R.J., Fanaroff, A.A., & Walsh, M.C. (2010) *Fanaroff and Martin's neonatal-perinatal medicine: Diseases of the fetus and infant* (9th ed., Vols. 1-2). St. Louis, MO: Elsevier Health Science.

McInerny, T., Adam, H., Campbell, D., & Kamat, D. (2008) *AAP textbook of pediatric primary care.* Elk Grove Village, IL: American Academy of Pediatrics.

Mengel, Mark and Schweibert, L. Peter. (2009) *Family Medicine: Ambulatory Care and Prevention.* New York, NY: McGraw-Hill Health.

Mulley, A. G., Goroll, A. H., & Mulley, A. G. (2009) *Primary care medicine: Office evaluation and management of the adult patient* (6th ed.). Philadelphia, PA: Lippincott Williams & Wilkins.

Nathan, L., Goodwin, T. M., Decherney, A. H., & Laufer, N. (2007) *Current diagnosis and treatment, obstetrics and gynecology* (10th ed.). New York, NY: McGraw-Hill/Appleton & Lange [Imprint].

Neinstein, L. S. (2008) *Adolescent health care: A practical guide* (5th ed.). Philadelphia, PA: Lippincott Williams & Wilkins.

Planned Parenthood Federation of America.(2001) *Manual of medical standards and guidelines.* New York, N.Y.: National Medical Division, Planned Parenthood Federation of America. Request in writing to: Kathy Coventry, Medical Communications Manager, 810 Seventh Avenue, New York, NY 10019.

Rakel, R. E. (2007). *Textbook of family medicine* (7th ed.). Philadelphia, PA: Saunders Elsevier.

Robertson, J., Shilkofski, N. (2009) *The Harriet Lane handbook: A manual for pediatric house officers* (18th ed.). Philadelphia, PA: Elsevier Mosby.

Rudolph, A.M., Karmel, R.K., Overby, K.J. (2002) *Rudolphs's fundamentals of pediatrics* (3rd ed.). New York, NY: McGraw-Hill Companies.

Sadock, B. J., & Sadock, V. A. (2007) *Kaplan and Sadock's synopsis of psychiatry* (10th ed.). Philadelphia, PA: Lipincott Williams & Wilkins.

Sadock, B., & Sadock, V. (2010) Kaplan & *Sadock's pocket handbook of clinical psychiatry* (5th ed.). Philadelphia, PA: Lippincott Williams and Wilkins.

Taketomo, C. K., Hodding, J. H., & Kraus, D. M. (2010) *Pediatric dosage handbook: International edition* (17th ed.). Hudson, OH: Lexi-Comp, Inc.

Tierney, L. M.,& Henderson, M. C. (2005) *The patient history: Evidence-based approach.* New York, NY: Lange Medical Books/McGraw-Hill Medical Pub. Division.

Tierney, L. M., McPhee, S. J., & Papadakis, M. A. (Editors.), (2010) *Current medical diagnosis & treatment.* New York, NY: Lange McGraw-Hill Medical.

Wallace, M. (2007) *Essentials of gerontological nursing.* New York, NY: Springer.

Yarbro, C. H.,Wujcik, D.,& Gobel, B. H. (Editors.). (2011) *Cancer nursing: Principles and practice* (7th ed.). Sudbury, MA: Jones and Bartlett.

Appendix C
Department of Health & Board of Nursing by State

Alabama: www.adph.org

Alaska: www.hss.state.ak.us

Arizona: www.azdhs.gov

Arkansas: www.healthy.arkansas.gov

California: www.dhs.ca.gov

Colorado: www.cdphe.state.co.us

Connecticut: www.ct.gov

Delaware: dpr.delaware.gov/boards/nursing

Florida: www.doh.state.fl.us

Georgia: www.sos.georgia.gov/plb/rn

Hawaii: hawaii.gov/dcca/pvl/boards/nursing

Idaho: ibn.idaho.gov

Illinois: www.idfpr.com/dpr/who/nurs

Indiana: www.in.gov/isdh

Iowa: www.state.ia.us/nursing

Kansas: www.ksbn.org

Kentucky: www.kbn.ky.gov

Louisiana: www.lsbn.state.la.us

Maine: www.maine.gov/boardofnursing

Maryland: www.dhmh.state.md.us

Massachusetts: www.mass.gov/?pageID=eohhs2agencylanding&L=4&L0=Home&L1
=Government&L2=Departments+and+Divisions&L3=Department+of+Public+Health&sid=Eeo
h hs2

Michigan: www.michigan.gov

Minnesota: www.state.mn.us/portal/mn/jsp/home.do?agency=NursingBoard

Mississippi: www.msdh.state.ms.us

Missouri: www.pr.mo.gov/nursing.asp

Montana: bsd.dli.mt.gov/license

Nebraska: www.hhs.state.ne.us/crl/nursing/rn-lpn/rn-lpn.htm

Nevada: www.oregon.gov/OSBN/index

New Hampshire: www.nh.gov/nursing

New Jersey: www.njconsumeraffairs.gov/nursing

New York: www.op.nysed.gov/prof/nurse

North Carolina: www.ncbon.com

North Dakota: www.ndbon.org

Ohio: www.nursing.ohio.gov

Oklahoma: www.ok.gov/nursing

Oregon: www.osbn.state.or.us

Pennsylvania: www.dos.state.pa.us

Rhode Island: www.health.state.ri.us/hsr/professions/nurses.php

South Carolina: www.llr.state.sc.us/pol/nursing

South Dakota: doh.sd.gov/boards/nursing

Tennessee: health.state.tn.us/boards/nursing

Texas: www.bne.state.tx.us

Utah: www.dopl.utah.gov/licensing/nurse

Vermont: www.vtprofessionals.org

Virginia: www.dhp.state.va.us/nursing

Washington: www.doh.wa.gov

West Virginia: www.wvrnboard.com

Wisconsin: drl.wi.gov

Wyoming: nursing-online.state.wy.us

Appendix D
List of DEA Offices

Alabama: www.justice.gov/dea/pubs/state_factsheets/alabama

Alaska: www.justice.gov/dea/pubs/state_factsheets/alaska

Arizona: www.justice.gov/dea/pubs/state_factsheets/arizona

Arkansas: www.justice.gov/dea/pubs/state_factsheets/arkansas

California: www.justice.gov/dea/pubs/state_factsheets/california

Colorado: www.justice.gov/dea/pubs/state_factsheets/colorado

Connecticut: www.justice.gov/dea/pubs/state_factsheets/connecticut

Delaware: www.justice.gov/dea/pubs/state_factsheets/delaware

Florida: www.justice.gov/dea/pubs/state_factsheets/florida

Georgia: www.justice.gov/dea/pubs/state_factsheets/georgia

Hawaii: www.justice.gov/dea/pubs/state_factsheets/hawaii

Idaho: www.justice.gov/dea/pubs/state_factsheets/idaho

Illinois: www.justice.gov/dea/pubs/state_factsheets/illinois

Indiana: www.justice.gov/dea/pubs/state_factsheets/indiana

Iowa: www.justice.gov/dea/pubs/state_factsheets/iowa

Kansas: www.justice.gov/dea/pubs/state_factsheets/kansas

Kentucky: www.justice.gov/dea/pubs/state_factsheets/kentucky

Louisiana: www.justice.gov/dea/pubs/state_factsheets/louisiana

Maine: www.justice.gov/dea/pubs/state_factsheets/maine

Maryland: www.justice.gov/dea/pubs/state_factsheets/maryland

Massachusetts: www.justice.gov/dea/pubs/state_factsheets/massachusetts

Michigan: www.justice.gov/dea/pubs/state_factsheets/michigan

Minnesota: www.justice.gov/dea/pubs/state_factsheets/minnesota

Mississippi: www.justice.gov/dea/pubs/state_factsheets/mississippi

Missouri: www.justice.gov/dea/pubs/state_factsheets/missouri

Montana: www.justice.gov/dea/pubs/state_factsheets/montana

Nebraska: www.justice.gov/dea/pubs/state_factsheets/nebraska

Nevada: www.justice.gov/dea/pubs/state_factsheets/nevada

New Hampshire: www.justice.gov/dea/pubs/state_factsheets/newhampshire

New Jersey: www.justice.gov/dea/pubs/state_factsheets/newjersey

New Mexico: www.justice.gov/dea/pubs/state_factsheets/newmexico

New York: www.justice.gov/dea/pubs/state_factsheets/newyork

North Carolina: www.justice.gov/dea/pubs/state_factsheets/northcarolina

North Dakota: www.justice.gov/dea/pubs/state_factsheets/northdakota

Ohio: www.justice.gov/dea/pubs/state_factsheets/ohio

Oklahoma: www.justice.gov/dea/pubs/state_factsheets/oklahoma

Oregon: www.justice.gov/dea/pubs/state_factsheets/oregon

Pennsylvania: www.justice.gov/dea/pubs/state_factsheets/pennsylvania

Rhode Island: www.justice.gov/dea/pubs/state_factsheets/rhodeisland

South Carolina: www.justice.gov/dea/pubs/state_factsheets/southcarolina

South Dakota: www.justice.gov/dea/pubs/state_factsheets/southdakota

Tennessee: www.justice.gov/dea/pubs/state_factsheets/tennessee

Texas: www.justice.gov/dea/pubs/state_factsheets/texas

Utah: www.justice.gov/dea/pubs/state_factsheets/utah

Vermont: www.justice.gov/dea/pubs/state_factsheets/vermont

Virginia: www.justice.gov/dea/pubs/state_factsheets/virginia

Washington: www.justice.gov/dea/pubs/state_factsheets/washington

West Virginia:www.justice.gov/dea/pubs/state_factsheets/westvirginia

Wiscowww.justice.gov/dea/pubs/state_factsheets/wisconsin

Wyoming: www.justice.gov/dea/pubs/state_factsheets/wyoming

Appendix E
List of local SBA Offices in your area

Alabama: www.sba.gov/localresources/district/al

Alaska: www.sba.gov/localresources/district/ak

Arizona: www.sba.gov/localresources/district/az

Arkansas: www.sba.gov/localresources/district/ar

California: www.sba.gov/localresources/district/ca

Colorado: www.sba.gov/localresources/district/co

Connecticut: www.sba.gov/localresources/district/ct

Delaware: www.sba.gov/localresources/district/de

Florida: www.sba.gov/localresources/district/fl

Georgia: www.sba.gov/localresources/district/ga

Hawaii:www.sba.gov/localresources/district/hi

Idaho: www.sba.gov/localresources/district/id

Illinois: www.sba.gov/localresources/district/il

Indiana: www.sba.gov/localresources/district/in

Iowa: www.sba.gov/localresources/district/ia

Kansas: www.sba.gov/localresources/district/ks

Kentucky: www.sba.gov/localresources/district/ky

Louisiana: www.sba.gov/localresources/district/la

Maine: www.sba.gov/localresources/district/me

Massachusetts: www.sba.gov/localresources/district/ma

Michigan: www.sba.gov/localresources/district/mi

Minnesota:www.sba.gov/localresources/district/mn

Mississippi:www.sba.gov/localresources/district/ms

Missouri:www.sba.gov/localresources/district/mo

Montana:www.sba.gov/localresources/district/mt

Nebraska:www.sba.gov/localresources/district/ne

Nevada: www.sba.gov/localresources/district/ne

New Hampshire: www.sba.gov/localresources/district/nh

New Jersey: www.sba.gov/localresources/district/nj

New Mexico: www.sba.gov/localresources/district/nm

New York: www.sba.gov/localresources/district/ny

North Carolina:www.sba.gov/localresources/district/nc

North Dakota:www.sba.gov/localresources/district/nd

Ohio:www.sba.gov/localresources/district/oh

Oklahoma:www.sba.gov/localresources/district/ok

Oregon:www.sba.gov/localresources/district/or

Pennsylvania: www.sba.gov/localresources/district/pa

Puerto Rico: www.sba.gov/localresources/district/pr

Rhode Island: www.sba.gov/localresources/district/ri

South Carolina: www.sba.gov/localresources/district/sc

South Dakota: www.sba.gov/localresources/district/sd

Tennessee:www.sba.gov/localresources/district/tn

Texas:www.sba.gov/localresources/district/tx

Utah: www.sba.gov/localresources/district/ut

Vermont: www.sba.gov/localresources/district/vt

Virginia:www.sba.gov/localresources/district/va

Washington:www.sba.gov/localresources/district/wa

Wisconsin:www.sba.gov/localresources/district/wi

Wyoming: www.sba.gov/localresources/district/wy

Appendix F
List of IRS Agencies

Alabama: www.irs.gov/localcontacts/article/0,,id=98236,00.

Alaska: www.irs.gov/localcontacts/article/0,,id=98253,00.

Arizona: www.irs.gov/localcontacts/article/0,,id=98256,00.

Arkansas: www.irs.gov/localcontacts/article/0,,id=98258,00.

California: www.irs.gov/localcontacts/article/0,,id=98259,00.

Colorado: www.irs.gov/localcontacts/article/0,,id=98261,00.

Connecticut: www.irs.gov/localcontacts/article/0,,id=98264,00.

Florida: www.irs.gov/localcontacts/article/0,,id=98268,00.

Georgia: www.irs.gov/localcontacts/article/0,,id=98270,00.

Hawaii: www.irs.gov/localcontacts/article/0,,id=98271,00.

Idaho: www.irs.gov/localcontacts/article/0,,id=98272,00.

Illinois: www.irs.gov/localcontacts/article/0,,id=98273,00.

Indiana: www.irs.gov/localcontacts/article/0,,id=98274,00.

Iowa: www.irs.gov/localcontacts/article/0,,id=98276,00.

Kansas: www.irs.gov/localcontacts/article/0,,id=98278,00.

Kentucky: www.irs.gov/localcontacts/article/0,,id=98281,00.

Louisiana: www.irs.gov/localcontacts/article/0,,id=98282,00.

Massachusetts: www.irs.gov/localcontacts/article/0,,id=98283,00.

Massachusetts: www.irs.gov/localcontacts/article/0,,id=98286,00.

Michigan: www.irs.gov/localcontacts/article/0,,id=98287,00.

Minnesota: www.irs.gov/localcontacts/article/0,,id=98289,00.

Mississippi: www.irs.gov/localcontacts/article/0,,id=98290,00.

Missouri: www.irs.gov/localcontacts/article/0,,id=98292,00.

Montana: www.irs.gov/localcontacts/article/0,,id=98295,00.

Nebraska: www.irs.gov/localcontacts/article/0,,id=98299,00.

Nevada: www.irs.gov/localcontacts/article/0,,id=98300,00.

New Hampshire:www.irs.gov/localcontacts/article/0,,id=98312,00.

New Mexico: www.irs.gov/localcontacts/article/0,,id=98317,00.

New York: www.irs.gov/localcontacts/article/0,,id=98318,00.

North Carolina: www.irs.gov/localcontacts/article/0,,id=98320,00.

North Dakota:www.irs.gov/localcontacts/article/0,,id=98321,00.l

Ohio: www.irs.gov/localcontacts/article/0,,id=98322,00.

Oklahoma: www.irs.gov/localcontacts/article/0,,id=98323,00.

Oregon: www.irs.gov/localcontacts/article/0,,id=98325,00.

Philadelphia: www.irs.gov/localcontacts/article/0,,id=98326,00.

Road Island: www.irs.gov/localcontacts/article/0,,id=98330,00.

South Carolina: www.irs.gov/localcontacts/article/0,,id=98332,00.

South Dakota: www.irs.gov/localcontacts/article/0,,id=98333,00.

Tennessee: www.irs.gov/localcontacts/article/0,,id=98336,00.

Texas: www.irs.gov/localcontacts/article/0,,id=98337,00.

Utah: www.irs.gov/localcontacts/article/0,,id=98338,00.

Vermont: www.irs.gov/localcontacts/article/0,,id=98340,00.

Virginia: www.irs.gov/localcontacts/article/0,,id=98342,00.

Washington: www.irs.gov/localcontacts/article/0,,id=98343,00.

West Virginia: www.irs.gov/localcontacts/article/0,,id=98346,00.

Wisconsin: www.irs.gov/localcontacts/article/0,,id=98349,00.

Wyoming: www.irs.gov/localcontacts/article/0,,id=98351,00.

References

- www.irs.gov/smallbiz
- http://www.op.nysed.gov/prof/nurse/np.htm#proc
- http://www.morebusiness.com/getting-started/incorporation/d934832501.brc
- www.cms.hhs.gov/nationalProvIdentstand
- www.health.ny.gov

38017259R00040

Made in the USA
Middletown, DE
04 March 2019